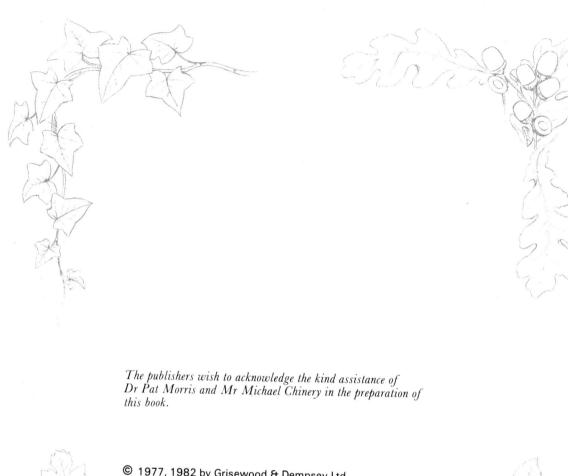

*The publishers wish to acknowledge the kind assistance of Dr Pat Morris and Mr Michael Chinery in the preparation of this book.*

© 1977, 1982 by Grisewood & Dempsey Ltd

Designed and produced by Grisewood & Dempsey Ltd, Elsley Court, 20-22 Great Titchfield Street, London W1

Published in 1982 in this edition by Galley Press, an imprint of W H Smith and Son Limited Registered No 237811 England. Trading as WHS Distributors, St John's House, East Street, Leicester, LE1 6NE

ISBN 0 86136 960 2

Printed and bound in Portugal by Printer Portuguesa, Sintra.

# The Fox

By Angela Sheehan
Illustrated by Bernard Robinson

Galley Press

The young vixen snuggled deep into the ditch, wrapped her warm tail around her nose and floated into a deep sleep. It was her second day away from home.

During the last two nights she had travelled a long way. She had crossed fields, jumped hedges, climbed hills and swum a stream. Now she was far from the woods where she had lived with her mother and the other cubs.

When she woke it was evening and time to continue her journey. But first she must eat. The night before she had only managed to steal some dry bread and bones from a village dustbin. But tonight she was near a farm and she could already smell the chickens.

The vixen had seen her mother raid a chicken run at home, so she knew what to do. She padded around the wire fence until she found a small gap. Then she scraped at the ground below and pushed up the wire with her nose. Now there was just enough room for her to squeeze through.

Once inside the run, the fox headed for the hen house. It was locked. But the fox had no need to open it. For there was one chicken sitting alone and asleep on top of the hen house.

As the fox approached, the chickens inside the hen house heard her and started to cluck. The noise woke the chicken outside and it flew into the air in a flurry of feathers. The fox leapt at the frightened chicken and brought it to the ground with one blow of her paw. Then she opened wide her mouth and sank her teeth into its tasty flesh.

After she had eaten the chicken, the fox ran on until she was far beyond the hills. By daybreak she was too tired to go any farther. She had reached a wood just like the one where she had lived as a cub. It would be a good place to make a new home.

At the edge of a large clearing deep inside the wood, the fox found a hole which opened into a long tunnel. At the end of the tunnel there was a grass-filled hollow. It made a perfect den. The fox was just settling in when she heard a scuffling noise from another tunnel and smelt an animal coming towards her. Quickly she scrambled out of the hole, and turned to see the striped face of an angry badger close behind her. The badger grunted as he chased the red-faced stranger from his set. It was not so easy to find a den after all.

Too tired to look any further, the fox curled up and went to sleep just where she was, beneath a hawthorn bush. Grasshoppers jumped high in the grass nearby as they woke to a new day. But even their loud chirping could not keep the sleepy vixen awake.

In the evening the fox explored the woods.
The scent of flowers, fruits and leaves filled her
nostrils. She could smell the rabbits that munched
the fresh grass and the mice that scampered
beneath the trees. But the smell she noticed most of
all was the scent of other foxes. Each night, she
followed their tracks by sniffing at the places they
marked with their scent. She could tell from their
scent whether they were vixens or dog-foxes, and
even how old they were.

Even though she had no real home of her own,
the fox had plenty to eat. She nibbled the thick
clusters of blackberries on the brambles and caught
the beetles and snails as they picked their way between

the prickles. She was even quick enough to catch the insects that hovered among the sweet fruits.

Each day she became more skilled as a hunter. She followed her prey slowly and silently, never allowing the wind to carry her scent towards the victim. And when she was near enough she pounced and killed swiftly. One of her favourite treats was to eat the frogs that hopped about by the stream at night.

One night she tried to catch a hedgehog that had also come to eat frogs. But unlike her mother she did not know how to unroll the prickly creature. She tried with all her might but her only reward was a sore paw.

After a while the weather became too cold for the fox to lie up just anywhere. So she set about finding a real home and making a place for herself in the wood.

She chose an old fox hole, near the rabbit warren. It would make a perfect earth. But first she had to clear out the rubbish that the last fox had left. There were old bones and scraps and feathers everywhere.

Once she had settled in the hole, she explored the area that was to be her home. She wanted to know every part of it. And she wanted the other foxes to know that she lived there, too. She covered the same path night after night. It took her more than an hour to walk all around her home area. As she went she marked certain tree stumps and clumps of grass with her scent. The other foxes would know from the smell that the place was hers and they would know too when she had passed by.

Now that she had a comfortable home of her own, the vixen would be able to have some cubs. But first she needed a mate. She knew where all the other foxes lived. At night when she heard them barking she often barked in reply. But she never really came very close to any of them. So at night she began to wail and scream and bark to let them know that she wanted a mate.

At first only a few farm dogs came to find
out what the noise was. But after some nights a
dog-fox that lived in a den in an old quarry heard
her wails. Even though his den was far away, he
hurried to answer her call. Every night from then on
he came to her. The two foxes played together in
mock battles and soon they learned to trust each
other enough to mate.

After they had mated the two foxes stayed in
their separate homes. But they still saw each other
as they paced the wintry woods looking for food.
Food was hard to find now for all the animals.
In spring and summer there were insects,
birds' eggs, and young animals, too weak to escape
from the foxes. But by the time winter came the
animals were fully grown; the insects were mostly
dead; the frogs were safely buried under the
ground; the squirrels were high in the trees; and
the mice were hidden in their burrows.

The fox had to be brave as well as cunning
to find enough to eat. She caught rabbits by
appearing to play harmlessly near them; attacked
deer twice her size; and stole ducks and geese from
the farm even during daylight. The ground by her
earth was littered with feathers and bones.

But winter did not last much longer.
The vixen's cubs were born just seven weeks after
she had mated. By then the first flowers were
beginning to bloom in the woods. But the young
cubs with their tightly-shut eyes could not see them.
They stayed curled up with their mother in the
earth, content to be suckled, washed and warmed
by her.

The vixen did not leave her cubs when they were first born. But she did not go hungry. Her mate brought her food until she could go out hunting herself. He also brought some food for the cubs, when they grew too big to live on their mother's milk.

Before they were a month old, the four cubs made their first trip outside. Their mother guarded them closely, keeping her ears and nose alert for any danger. The cubs enjoyed being in the open where they could run about and play together, and see all the new sights, smell all the new smells and hear all the new sounds.

Every evening they went out to play. They chased flies, attacked feathers in the wind, pounced on each other and fought for bones. One of their favourite games was trying to catch their mother's tail as she whisked it from side to side.

As they grew, they learned more games. Instead of giving them their food their mother would hide it and leave them to sniff it out for themselves. The smallest cub never found the food first. He began to be very hungry. But the others grew more and more clever. Soon they would be able to catch food for themselves.

But they were still too young to go far into the woods. Their mother watched all the time they were out. One bark from her would bring them all running back to the safety of the earth. And when she went out hunting herself she made sure they were asleep. She also made sure that no enemies could catch her scent and follow her home.

But the fox's earth was too near the rabbit warren to be safe. Often men came from the farm to shoot the rabbits. The cubs ran from the sound of the guns, but their mother knew that they were in real danger. So she left her earth by night and took the whole family deeper into the wood.

She found a fine hole right on the edge of the badger's set. The badgers had stopped using the hole long before so they did not mind the foxes taking it over. Soon the family had settled in. Within days the badgers' set began to look a mess. The tidy badgers always cleared their rubbish away, but the foxes left theirs scattered everywhere.

When they were two months old, the cubs went out hunting with their mother. There was a lot to learn; so many different animals to catch and so many different ways to catch them. They also had to learn where to look. Finding nesting birds and taking their eggs was easy, except for the small cub. He always chased the mother bird as it flew away, while the other cubs ate the eggs. He would never be a good hunter. He only got any food when he found the body of an animal that was already dead.

The others soon found it easy to catch rabbits and voles and even fast-moving mice. They had learned to pounce with their paws and not snap at the creatures with their jaws.

One day the small cub went out by himself early in the evening to look for food. All he could see were pretty flowers and all he could hear was the sound of buzzing. One clump of foxgloves was covered in bumblebees. They smelled so good that the hungry cub ran at them and tried to eat them. But they turned out not to be so tasty. One by one they stung him furiously on the nose. He squealed and ran home to his mother as fast as he could. He would never be big and brave like the others.

But the cub could not live with his mother forever. Soon the other three cubs left home. They were ready to go into the world: perhaps to make a long journey to a new place as their mother had done; perhaps to be killed by a car on the road, shot by a farmer, or chased by huntsmen; perhaps to bring up a litter of cubs for themselves. Even the smallest fox must take his chance and try to fend for himself.

So the young cub left the earth, last of all. His mother was tired after bringing up her family. She needed a rest before she had her next litter.

# More About Foxes

The fox in the story is the red fox. It lives in Europe, North Africa, parts of Asia and in North America. Other foxes live in other parts of the world. The arctic fox has a white coat to match the snowy lands in which it lives. The small sandy coloured fennec fox lives in the desert.

## Where foxes live

Foxes do not have a particular home except when they are breeding. During the summer, foxes lie up anywhere, in dens. These may be in thickets, in ditches, or among rocks. In winter they find (never dig) an underground home, called an earth. The fox lays claim to the surrounding area by marking 'posts' with a strong scent mixed in with its urine. The area is called a 'home range'. Often several fox ranges overlap and the foxes use the same tracks. They communicate with each other by exchanging barks, and leaving scent messages.

## Cunning as a fox

The fox is justly famous for its cunning, especially for its habit of 'charming' rabbits. It leaps about playfully near them and shows no sign of having seen them. The watching rabbits cannot take their eyes off the dancing fox and stay rooted to the spot, until suddenly the fox pounces.

Unlike rabbits, farmers know all about the fox's cunning. They know that it will watch and wait until the right moment. Then it will kill every hen in a run if it can find a way in, or savagely attack new born lambs. That is why farmers shoot foxes.

But foxes do not always kill for food. They will happily eat the bodies of animals already dead (carrion) or eat leftovers that they find in dustbins. More and more foxes are now making their homes on the outskirts of towns where there is plenty of rubbish to scavenge. When foxes find more food than they can eat, they sometimes bury some to eat later.

**Ears** are large to collect as much sound as possible. An alert fox has its ears pricked. It can hear even better than a dog.

**Eyes** are not as important as nose and ears, but fox can see movement well at night. Look at the photograph on the opposite page.

**Tail** The fox's tail is called a brush. It helps it to balance; to signal to other foxes; and to keep warm, using it like a scarf.

**Nose** The fox's sense of smell is very keen. Its wet nose enables it to tell which way the wind is blowing, so it knows exactly where any smell is coming from.

**Teeth** Long ones at the front for tearing meat and sharp side ones for slicing it.

**Legs** Strong legs and feet for running. The fox does not run especially fast, but it can run far at a steady speed.

**The body of a red fox**

killed so that the farm animals are safe. But there are less cruel ways of killing them.

## Keeping watch

Although foxes are cunning hunters, they are easy prey for fox watchers because they leave so many signs that people can see. Outside any fox hole you will find the leftovers of their food. The tracks they make and the 'posts' they mark are easy to find and follow. You can track them from their droppings, too. But remember that the fox can hear and smell you coming long before you see it. So, if you want to see a fox you must be very patient, or lucky. You may see one in your garden, or from the window of a train. Foxes nowadays often lie up by the railway tracks.

A family of fox cubs, their eyes lit up by the flash of a camera. Their eyes shine brightly because foxes have special 'mirrors' in their eyes. The mirrors reflect light so that there seems to be more light than there is, and this helps the fox to see better at night.

## Faithful father

A female fox is ready to breed in her first year, and has one litter each year. Her cubs are born in winter and they leave home in summer. While she is suckling them, her mate brings her food even though he does not share the earth. Many people deny that dog-foxes do this, but others say that they have seen them.

## Tally ho

This is the cry of the huntsman as he sets off with horses and hounds to chase and kill a single fox. People have hunted in this way, wearing special pink (red) coats, for centuries. Today many people would like hunting to be banned. There are too many foxes and some must be

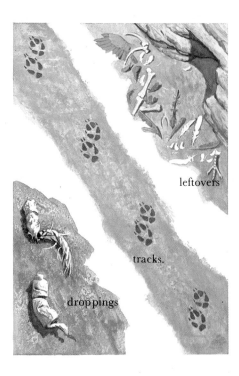

leftovers

tracks.

droppings

**Some things to look for when tracking a fox**